Tiffany

Lee Ann Sifuentes

To order additional copies of this book, contact:
Xlibris
1-888-795-4274
www.Xlibris.com
Orders@Xlibris.com

ISBN: Softcover   978-1-7960-6978-5
       Hardcover   978-1-7960-6979-2
       EBook   978-1-7960-6977-8

Print information available on the last page

Rev. date: 11/05/2019

Tiffany

Autism:

A developmental disorder of variable severity that is characterized by difficulty in social interaction and communication and by restricted or repetitive patterns of thought and behavior.

Tiffany

likes to play at home, or at the park.

Tiffany

likes to go for a car ride in the dark.

likes to spin around with her brother.

Jump on the
trampoline with
her sister,

Or swing
outside with
her mother.

Tiffany

likes to prance.

Tiffany

likes to dance.

Tiffany

likes to kick off
her pants.

Tiffany

likes to sing her abcs, she also counts her 123s.

Tiffany

likes puzzles parties and princesses.

Tiffany

**likes wearing
cute dresses.**

Tiffany

likes stemming.

She'll hold her hand on her hair bun and hum.

Sometimes *Tiffany* likes to be a beach bum.

She loves the water and wants to go for a swim.

Daddy holds her hand and *Tiffany* jumps in.

Tiffany

likes to splash
in the waves.

Tiffany laughs

Tiffany plays

Tiffany can swim for days.

Printed in the United States
By Bookmasters